FAITH FOR THE G●LD

TRAVIS C. JENNINGS

ME
WE

MORE EXCELLENT
WAY ENTERPRISES

Publisher:
MEWE, LLC
Lithonia, GA
www.mewellc.com

First Edition
ISBN: 978-0-9988281-2-1

Library of Congress Number: 2017905894

For Worldwide Distribution
Printed in the USA

To the 'no names' who are now the 'new names,' to the movers and shakers who know that 'no' is not the end, yet the beginning of negotiations, to the emergent voices that are evolving in their fields of expertise—may you forever be world changers, and global shifter for the glory of God.

TABLE OF CONTENTS

Acknowledgements vii

Introduction ix

Chapter 1: Potential Faith 1

    Play #1: "Get Your Head in the Game" 2

    Play #2: "Show Me What You Got" 5

    Play #3: "Mind Over Matter" 9

Chapter 2: Faith to Go the Distance 21

    Play #1: "Built to Last" 22

    Play #2: Man Up" 29

    Play #3: "He's God Game" 42

    Play #4: "No 'I' in Team" 54

Chapter 3: The Saga 57

    Play #1: "High Level Intensity Training" 58

    Play #2: Winning with You've Got 62

    Play #3: "Play Smarter Not Harder" 67

Chapter 4: Olympic Faith 71

    Play #1: "Can't Stop, Won't Stop" 72

    Play #2: "You Are What You Eat" 75

    Play #3: "Known by the Company You Keep" 77

About the Author 81

ACKNOWLEDGMENTS

To God be the glory for the things that He has done! It is He who I first thank for endowing me with the grace necessary to complete the assignment on my life. It is in Him that I live, move, and exist, and would have it be no other way. The journey to this day has not been the easiest, but with God's love, strength, and protection it has certainly not been the hardest. Thank you Lord, for your power and your nature being made manifest in my life daily; for without it none of this would be possible.

I further thank my precious wife and the mother of all my children, Stephanie LaShaun Jennings. Over 18 years ago, you made the decision to love me as your husband. You chose to leave what you knew behind, to follow me, as I followed Christ. You have also chosen to submit to the vision, support the assignment, and serve alongside me in ministry. You are my queen and my glory here on Earth, and I love you! You, along with our children, continue to be the driving force behind me being better than yesterday. You pray with me, and for me as I go forth in the things of God.

It is my chief joy to make you Stephanie, and our beautiful children: Travis, Briona, Daja, Destiny, and David Christopher happy and forever proud to call me, husband, dad, and pastor.

Lastly, but certainly not least, I especially thank the partners of the Harvest Tabernacle Church—a church like no other! I appreciate every vision partner, torch bearer, and son and daughter of the ministry for their continued support and service in helping me gather the End-Time Harvest. God's word lets us know that without a vision the people perish, and while this is true, I too know, that without a people the vision will also perish. I sincerely thank you, my church, for releasing me to do, and supporting me as I do, what God has called.

INTRODUCTION

Faith is biblically identified by the Apostle Paul as, *"the assurance (the confirmation, the title deed) of the things [we] hope for, being the proof of things [we] do not see and the conviction of their reality [faith perceiving as real fact what is not revealed to the senses]"* (Hebrews 11:1 AMP).

At this point, you may be wondering, "What does knowing this have to do with me? I know this scripture like the back of my hand. I know faith! I have faith!"

Great! I'm glad you have faith, and I'm glad you know God's Word concerning it. Most of all, I'm glad you asked that question!

Prophetically, in the timing of God, the body of Christ is where He is raising up an All-Star team. It's going to take a great level of faith for you to make the draft. The wisest person has at least an inkling, a knowing, a discernment of what his or her field is. Your field may not be the same as mine, and my field may not be yours, but God has already designed and assigned a field for each of us to serve for His glory.

1 Peter tells us that *"Ye are a chosen generation, a royal priesthood, a holy nation, a peculiar people, that should show forth the praises of Him who has called us out of darkness into His marvelous light"* (1 Peter 2:9). Romans adds that creation is eagerly waiting for God's children to be revealed (See Romans 8:19).

Now is the season when the earth is waiting for the manifested sons! A Son in this context is not related to gender, but to our position. No longer does the earth want carbon copies. It is waiting for the originals – for the ones who have been created by God to step into His glorious design for their lives.

The good news is, "The wait is coming to an end because now is the time! This is the time when you are going to do what you were perfectly created to do, and you will dominate in your field of expertise!"

Usually, when you think of All-Stars, you automatically think of sports and athletes. While this is accurate, it is incomplete. All-Star teams are a collection of star performers. Now keep in mind that Jesus is the bright and morning star (See Revelation 22:16). The Bible tells us that as He was in the earth, so are we (See 1 John 4:17). Therefore, you are a star!

You may not know it yet, but you are a star, and something is burning inside your heart. You might think it's gas or indigestion, but it is neither of the two. It is the creative power of God inside you. You have star-like qualities. That's why you dream big, see big, sing big, speak big—you even have big hair! You have star power, and star power can't be hidden. It's going to shine. In fact, you can't touch it. It'll burn you. This is a season when people will not be able to touch you.

The title of All-Star is often bestowed on an individual who consistently performs at a high-performance level in their field. They are the best athletes at their positions from all teams in a league or region. Simply put, they are the best of the best at what they do! All-Stars are teamed up with other individuals within their region who can perform at a similar level of quality in the same field. All-Star players are top performers who are collectively dubbed with the title "All-Star Team" and given the task to represent their field and region during the All-Star games.

This is what God is doing with the body of Christ. We are in a time when God is raising up the star performers. I am not referring to movie stars or TV personalities. God's star performers are those who have really been in the training process where God has been developing, and putting muscle on their bones. These are stronger on their knees than all the forces of evil in this world system. These have discovered the power of God is just as real for them today as it was centuries ago for Moses, for Elijah, for Peter or Paul today as it was centuries ago for Moses, for Elijah, for Peter or Paul. These are the ones who work harder for the Lord because they KNOW that the answer to prayer is on its way. They aren't afraid of life's tests and trials because they understand it as a part of the training of champions.

Some of them were involved in sports during earlier times of life. They recall how the coach made them run laps even after a fierce practice session. They thought they couldn't make ten laps, until they were at the ninth one and heard the coach announce, "Only six more to go, guys! Let's not stop at ten. Let's push it a little harder and make it fifteen!" At first, they thought it was impossible, but by the end of the season, they were running twenty laps or more at the end of practice.

Now, they are applying some of that same understanding to what their spiritual Coach is doing. He doesn't always make it easy, but He does always make it worth it. He knows what it takes to make a true champion who has faith for the gold.

He is preparing the best of the best to represent their field and the Kingdom of God in the game called life. Be warned. It will not be an instantaneous occurrence, but it will happen swiftly! All-Star players must undergo and persevere through numerous tests and obstacles. These training exercises are designed to display and challenge their abilities; it will be no different for you.

Your faith must be more than the passive, flabby faith of those who spend their days lying on the couch, eating potato chips, and watching sports heroes win the gold. The faith of an All-Star champion is a disciplined, determined, and decisive faith. It seizes the future and pulls it into the present. It is powerful and dynamic, living and life-changing faith.

Trying to live the Christian life without knowing how to apply our faith is like a person who is totally paralyzed. Can you picture that image? Imagine yourself, locked in a body that refuses to obey what your mind is telling it to do. Although you are a living, thinking, feeling person, your abilities have been so limited that you aren't able to demonstrate your love for family and friends. You may be intellectually brilliant, but physically incapable of fully exercising your abilities. The Apostle James said, *"Faith without works is dead"* (James 2:14-26). Unless our faith is functioning in our daily lives, it cannot make a real difference for us or those we love.

God has chosen you for His winning team. He didn't choose you without having a clear plan for what He wants to accomplish with your life. He called you to be victorious over your opposition. He didn't design your life to be a tragedy of failures. He knows His own purposes and power. He knows you, including all the weaknesses you don't yet know you have. He intends to turn those weaknesses of yours into trophy-winning assets because his strength is made perfect in weakness (See 2 Corinthians 12:9).

Please understand that I am not coaching you through something that I have not worked through myself. Would you go to a dentist who doesn't have any teeth? Would you take marriage advice from a couple who aren't married? You should not have anyone teaching you who has no expertise on the matter at hand.

Within these pages, you'll find that you're reading a practical guide filled with effective strategies and techniques to build your faith muscles. You'll be equipped with more than the strength to play the game of life well. You will be empowered to win! It's called All-Star faith, and you're going to need it, because you've been drafted by God to "Go for the Gold!"

CHAPTER 1

Potential Faith

FAITH FOR THE GOLD

Play #1

★ ★ ★

"GET YOUR HEAD IN THE GAME"

At any given time, can you successfully execute in your field? Are you confident that you will achieve gold status every time?

If your answer is "No," "I'm not sure," or if you were hesitant to answer, then you're where you should be, studying play one! It's okay. By the end of this training, you'll know how to win in this game. Your potential faith will be activated.

As we start with the basics, you should know you've been given responsibilities. You have been given an order, direction, and instruction. These were not self-assigned because players cannot self-assign themselves. Someone greater, the coach, must assign you to a purpose and give you a commission.

God is the One who has developed the game plan and given to us an assignment. It has been prophetically declared that we are going to lead in our field of expertise. So, confess boldly, "I'm anointed for my assignment!"

Now that you've committed to your anointed assignment, we'll begin the transformation process of becoming an All-Star player with All-Star faith. It all starts with the head!

The first thing that must be enhanced is your thought pattern. Your thoughts must be redirected because transformation only happens when the mind embraces the needed changes. In other words, you've got to get your head in the game. *"Do not conform to the pattern of this world, but be transformed by the renewing of your mind. Then you will be able to test and approve what God's will is--his good, pleasing and perfect will"* (Romans 12:2). The other team, the world system, is trying to play with your head to get you to yield to their deceptions.

Dr. Jack J. Lesyk is the Director of the Ohio Center for Sports Psychology and Sport Psychologist for a team you may know called the Cleveland Cavaliers. Dr. Lesyk has compiled a list of nine mental skills required by all successful athletes. Remarkably, these skills correspond to aspects of the mental transformation God desires for His All-Star team. They are:

1) Choose and maintain a positive attitude.

2) Maintain a high level of self-motivation.

3) Set high, realistic goals.

4) Deal effectively with people.

5) Use positive self-talk.

6) Use positive mental imagery.

7) Manage anxiety effectively.

8) Manage their emotions effectively.

9) Maintain concentration.

Most college and professional coaches know that the success of their team is not entirely a matter of physical conditioning or strength training. They understand that players must be mentally prepared before they set foot on the field of competition, regardless of the sport. The same principle applies for other non-athletic performers such as ballet dancers and musicians. Success requires a level of mental discipline and refinement that is unknown to the amateurs who only dream of becoming a champion.

Your mind must fully embrace the fact that you're working with "big stuff" even if no one else believes it. You have been designed to handle anything that comes your way. You are not inferior to anyone and should not stand subservient to anyone, especially those with a superiority complex.

> *Major doors of opportunity are going to be opened to you...*

God didn't design you for inferiority. Major doors of opportunity are going to be opened to you, and if you think yourself as inadequate, you're going to miss it.

Regardless of the opposition or the negativity of those who surround you, you must be able to sustain a positive attitude, knowing that you have been chosen as part of God's team, one that is predestined for greatness. No strategy that any enemy has can overcome the Master plan.

Be sure of this fact: your natural self does not qualify you for the All-Star team, but it is the God given potential working within you (See Philippians 2:13). *"I have strength for all things in Christ Who empowers me [I am ready for anything and equal to anything through Him Who [a]infuses inner strength into me; I am [b]self-sufficient in Christ's sufficiency]* (Philippians 4:13). It is the greater one in you who wakes up and faces the challenge every time (See 1 John 4:4). How can you become discouraged or depressed when you know that you have been equipped with divine resources that cannot be defeated?

Play #2

"SHOW ME WHAT YOU'RE WORKING WITH"

We're still working the mind, but now we're shifting from the conditioning to the warm up. The first play was designed to bring you into a state of awareness. Now we are ready to start engaging your mental muscles in the process. Show me what you're working with.

To be an effective player on this team, each player must know, understand, and own their potential. **According to www.thefreedictionary.com,** potential is "that which is capable of being but not yet in existence."

With that fact in mind, the Holy Spirit reveals that God-given potential is the raw material, the untapped energy that enables us to win every time.

You are working with God-given potential. Understandably, this may be a bit difficult for you to believe, but it's true. Consider this analogy:

There is a driver – a safe driver who is cautious, wears his seatbelt, and always drives the speed limit. The driver knows that the car can move faster; however, he intentionally flows with traffic in a way that doesn't test the vehicle's limits.

Now, this same driver gets home and finds that his baby has a fever of 107°F. With a mindset of urgency, the cautious driver, who usually goes the speed limit, jumps in the car and proceeds to drive faster than norm.

5

He is going with the flow of traffic, yet driving aggressively to get to the Emergency Room. This driver is now pushing the limits of the vehicle because he knows that the car has the potential to go past the speed he is accustomed to driving.

Through this analogy, you find that you have the potential to go past your comfort level, but you seldom do so because of what you think and see. Truthfully, you have more in you that can be used. **The ceiling you've been living under is a false reality that hinders understanding of how far you can really go. It is said that seeing is believing, however true achievement comes from how your mind interprets what you see. The true reality is that you're under a drop ceiling, but you have the ability to break pass that ceiling.**

It's not your limit. Once you pass the ceiling, you still have a roof, and once you pass the roof, you still have the sky and once you pass the sky, you still have the stars.

In life, you must experience a time when you ask yourself probing questions about what is possible for you. As you look around, you observe the scope of human potential, and it causes you to wonder what is possible for you. This is nothing out of the norm. However, if you're not careful, you will end up defining your potential based on the words of man and not on the Word of God.

Potential has to be explained by the Scriptures, or it will be exploited by the secular world. Many talents and gifts for the Kingdom have fallen captive to the world. This happens because individuals are working their talents and gifts with little to no knowledge of their potential. If you're

*66 **Potential has to be explained by the Scriptures...** 99*

operating in talents and gifts without someone prophetically explaining to you their purpose and power of them, then you're open for the world to exploit those gifts for its wicked gain.

Somewhere along life's journey we allow our thinking to be held captive by imposed standards, stereotypes, and statistics. Who told you what you could have? How many people have you allowed to tell you what is possible for you? Where did you get the limitations in your thinking?

Oftentimes, unbeknownst to us, we allow others to define our potential and limit it and us to their personal thoughts. So how do you start to live outside of imposed standards, stereotypes, and statistics? The answer can be found in your honest response to three simple questions.

1. Did the individual have the right to define your potential – the scope of what you are capable of doing, having, and becoming?

2. What was their motive in defining your potential?

3. Did they tell you the truth?

The truthful answers to these questions could very well be earth shattering. I should say, 'limitation shattering!' If you stir up enough curiosity to ask the right probing questions, you are well on your way to successfully playing the game of life and winning the gold at the end of it all.

The right to define a person's potential belongs to God. He is the only authoritative figure with the right to define your capabilities. In the practical sense, it is the exclusive right of the maker of a thing to define how that particular thing best functions. God is our maker and therefore reserves the right to define our potential.

"Know ye that the Lord, he is God: it is he that hath made us and not we ourselves; we are his people, and the sheep of his pasture" (Psalm 100:3).

Play #3

★ ★ ★

"MIND OVER MATTER"

We're shifting again! The mental workout will intensify because we're adding weights.

The only way you're going to build muscle is through resistance. You've made it through the conditioning and the warm up and now you're ready for insight into your opponent's game plan. The Bible says, *"Lest Satan should get an advantage of us: for we are not ignorant of his devices"* (2 Corinthians 2:11).

As God's draft pick, you must know that your opponents are real, and they are striving to make you lose. You'll have to play the game smarter and not harder. Every advantage you get over your opponent will benefit you as you go for the gold.

Satan and his imps conspire for you to fail. By knowing what you're up against, you will be able to effectively engage your mind to win. **You cannot allow yourself to be ignorant about the game plan that Satan's team will use against you.**

The greatest football players don't just master their own game plan. They watch countless hours of footage, studying every move of the key players of the opposing team. They watch every offensive and defensive play and how various players work their position assignments. They learn the weaknesses of that team and are ready for an opportunity to exploit those weaknesses on the field.

Throughout the All-Star games, our opponents will be working

9

overtime to make sure we're content when we should be commissioned, satisfied when we should be shifters, and resting when we should be revolutionaries. It's a scheme, the satanic plot of our opponent, the devil.

Four Diabolical Plays of the Enemy

During the All –Star games, the devil strikes with four diabolical plays: experimentation, exploitation, evaluation, and expectation.

Experimentation

We are all guilty of trying new things. In our past, we did things with little or no knowledge of the consequence it would have on our future. It is ignorance at its best. The opponent uses the results of your experimentation to destroy your belief in God for anything. **In the midst of key plays, he will try to convince you that you have a better idea about how to score–better than the game plan and the assignment that your coach has given you. You were trained to stay in the pocket and watch for the tight end to break left, but you decided to get the first down by rolling out to the right and hit the wide receiver. Looks like a great plan for a moment or two…just before you get sacked!**

We never have a better game plan than our Coach. He alone can see into the future and know how we should handle difficult plays. That's why we must listen and learn from Him and then execute His plan instead of experimenting with our own.

Exploitation

If he's unable to completely take you out with his first scheme, he proceeds to strike with the play of exploitation. This attack is set up to have those who are supposed to help you, hurt you instead. The results of this tactic are oftentimes more intense than that of experimentation. The opponent's goal is to use the results of this attack to cause disbelief and deplete your drive.

What quarterback hasn't had occasions when his defensive line seems to evaporate at just the wrong moment? What relay racer hasn't held a lead, only to see it disappear when his partner dropped the baton? What eager young believer hasn't seen seasoned Christians compromise or cruelly criticize the man of God who has faithfully proclaimed the truth of the Word? Or maybe a brother or sister boldly declares that they don't see how God could use someone who has the weaknesses you do – nothing could be more discouraging,

Evaluation

Surviving those previous two attacks are major accomplishments. I'm sure you have the scars to prove what you've been through; but there are still more blows to come. At this stage of the game, your opponent will intensify his attacks. He's now going to strike with evaluation. During this ploy, you compare yourself to another person's potential. This is one of your opponent's trickiest schemes; because he's working through you and not others to give the false perception that others are living and doing better than you.

His goal here is for you to evaluate and compare yourself against an unrealistic standard – another's potential. This results in your continuously giving yourself a failing grade. Realistically, you need to leave your teammates' potential alone and tap into your own.

Many believers have spiritual heroes, either in the Word or in their daily lives. They've heard and seen the incredible accomplishments of these warriors of faith. They've seen amazing prayers answered, healing and deliverance, and supernatural provision…all of it happening in the lives of those heroes, but not in their own. They begin to find fault with themselves and to lower their estimation of what God might do with them. They begin to doubt that the signs and wonders recorded in the Bible are intended to ever be part of their own experience.

Expectation

As if that isn't enough, there's still one more attack to go; expectations! During this attack, you find that the things you thought would work, didn't! Because of apparent failures, you no longer trust in the system of the Kingdom. This is diabolical at its best because you're now your worst enemy. Case in point, you paid your tithes for thirty days and falsely expect a million-dollar check would show up at your address in thirty days. When it doesn't, you become mad at God, when honestly you should be mad at your opponent for giving you the false expectation.

Psalm 62:5 reminds us, "My soul, wait thou only upon God; for my expectation is from him." We cannot afford to have misplaced expectations because they are always false. Furthermore, we must clearly understand what God's will and promises include and exclude. We cannot allow ourselves to indulge in falsehood when each of us has access to the living Word of God.

I'm certain that you have suffered through one, if not all of these attacks. It's quite possible that one, if not all of them knocked the wind right out of you initially. Fortunately for you, God is aware of this. He stays abreast of each attack our opponent uses to defeat us. Being the coach that He is, God embedded in each of His players everything necessary to counteract the attacks of their opponent.

God is not in the habit of training us, preparing us, and equipping us for nothing. All the years that were spent praying, fasting, believing, and even going to school weren't for nothing!

You are getting ready to dominate in your field of expertise, and God has just removed the false reality. Your ceiling is higher than you thought it to be. You've got another hundred years in you. You are not dying anytime soon because you've got about five more mountains you're about to conquer!

> " *You are getting ready to dominate in your field of expertise...* "

It is possible that the thought is inconceivable to your natural mind, but players on this team do not lose. **God Himself has declared that we are** *"more than conquerors through him that loved us"* (Romans 8:37).

"How's that?" you ask. It's this simple!

Four Fundamental Potential Levels

Every player on God's team has four fundamental potential levels that cause them to conquer, and you are not exempted.

Covenant Potential

Your covenant relationship with the Lord affords you privileges. The grace of God was placed upon you when you accepted the draft and became a part of the spiritual family. Tap into it!

In your New Covenant relationship, you are not alone, and you are not powerless. God has given you the covenant token of His indwelling Spirit who has all power. Your covenant potential is beyond human imagination. It as boundless as your Covenant Partner. Our covenant potential is not based on our strength or ability. No, we have a source that is reserved for those who are in covenant with Almighty God. He is our strength when our own has faded. Isaiah 40:13 assures us, "…they that wait upon the LORD shall renew their strength; they shall mount up with wings as eagles; they shall run, and not be weary; and they shall walk, and not faint."

Your potential is unknown to the world and even to yourself, but fully known to your Creator. You are predestined to accomplish great things. Just listen to how the Apostle Paul explained the privileged position of those shaped by the hand of God. He wrote, *"For we are his workmanship, created in Christ Jesus unto good works, which God hath before ordained that we should walk in them"* (Ephesians 2:10). God has a game plan that perfectly fits how He has designed you.

Confessed Potential

Your confessed potential refers to the results of the intentional faith you exercise for greater results.

> *For verily I say unto you, That whosoever shall say to the mountain, Be thou removed, and be thou cast into the sea; and shall not doubt in his heart, but shall believe that those things which he saith shall come to pass, he shall have whatsoever he saith. Therefore, I say unto you, What things soever ye desire, when ye pray, believe that ye receive them, and ye shall have them* (Mark 11:23-24).

Connected Potential

When you are properly connected, the development of your potential is greatly increased. It is where the undeniable order of God teams up for a mentoring relationship.

> *And the Lord was with Joseph, and he was a*

14

prosperous man; and he was in the house of his master the Egyptian. And his master saw that the Lord was with him, and that the Lord made all that he did to prosper in his hand. And Joseph found grace in his sight, and he served him: and he made him overseer over his house, and all that he had he put into his hand. And it came to pass from the time that he had made him overseer in his house, and over all that he had, that the Lord blessed the Egyptian's house for Joseph's sake; and the blessing of the Lord was upon all that he had in the house, and in the field. And he left all that he had in Joseph's hand; and he knew not ought he had, save the bread which he did eat. And Joseph was a goodly person, and well favoured (Genesis 39:2-6).*

God will place you so that you are connected to your destiny, giving you opportunities to develop and to apply your emerging potentials. Joseph had been sold as a slave, but that did not define him. In the sovereign game plan of God, Joseph was given the chance to demonstrate the character, convictions, and competence that God had instilled in him.

Whatever your circumstances, whether they are positions of power and privilege or humble surroundings where your potential is hidden from the eyes of men, you are still connected to God's agenda and to the people He has chosen to equip you for future achievements.

Confounding Potential

Obedience has the potential to position us in places of opportunity, where we can be more, do more, and have more!

And saw two ships standing by the lake: but the fishermen were gone out of them, and were washing their nets. And he entered into one of the ships, which was Simon's, and prayed him that he would thrust out a little from the land. And he sat down, and taught the people out of the ship. Now when he had left speaking, he said unto Simon, Launch out into the deep, and let down your nets for a draught. And Simon answering said unto him, Master, we have toiled all the night, and have taken nothing: nevertheless at thy word I will let down the net. And when they had this done, they inclosed a great multitude of fishes: and their net brake (Luke 5:2-6).

Potential, accurately defined, is necessary for anyone who is going for the gold. God knew this, and that is why He made it so that we have the Bible. The Bible is God's presentation of what He purposed for mankind and is a historical documentation of mankind living out those expectations. With biblical evidence, we're able to see that God has much higher expectations for us than we usually have for ourselves. Therefore, you should stand assured that God has an amazingly incredible plan for you. **The wisdom of God always confounds the wisdom of man. His ways and His thoughts are always greater and higher than ours (See Isaiah 55:8-9).**

If you are still seeking God for your own purpose, you are not a manifested son yet. If you are still praying about your purpose, you are not a manifested son yet. If you are doing something that has nothing to do with your purpose or your assignment, you are not a manifested son yet. The earth if still waiting on you.

If you know your purpose say this with me, but say it like you believe it, "I am so glad that I am in my purpose, I know my assignment, and I know my destiny. I am a manifested son. The earth is no longer awaiting me, because I am here." The fact that you are reading this prophetic book right now, proves you are a manifested son. You understand that your purpose and destiny have everything to do with the Word of God being ministered to you.

However, if for some reason you're unable to take my word for it, take God's Word for it. He has revealed it through multiple scriptures.

All-Star Mind Conditioning Scriptures

For I know the thoughts that I think towards you, saith the Lord. Thoughts of peace, and not of evil; to give you an expected end (Jeremiah 29:11).

★ ★ ★

Remember the former things of old: for I am God, and there is none else; I am God, and there is none like me. Declaring the end from the beginning, and from ancient time the things that are not yet done, saying, My counsel shall stand, and I will do all my pleasure: Calling a ravenous bird from the east, the man that executeth my counsel from a far country: yea, I have spoken it, I will also bring it to pass; I have purposed it, I will also do it (Isaiah 46:9-11).

★ ★ ★

Therefore, my beloved brethren, be ye steadfast, unmovable, always abounding in the work of the Lord, forasmuch as ye know that your labour is not in vain in the Lord (1 Corinthians 15:58).

★ ★ ★

17

So God created man in his own image, in the image of God he created he him; male and female he created he them. And God blessed them, and God said unto them, be fruitful and multiply, and replenish the earth, and subdue it: and have dominion over the fish of the sea, and over the fowl of the air, and over every living thing that moveth upon the earth (Genesis 1:27-28).

———★ ★ ★———

Now unto him that is able to do exceeding abundantly above all that we ask or think, according to the power that worketh in us; unto him be glory in the church by Christ Jesus throughout all ages, world without end. Amen (Ephesians 3:20-21).

———★ ★ ★———

And the Lord said, Behold, the people is one, and they have all one language; and this they begin to do: and now nothing will be restrained from them, which they have imagined to do (Genesis 11:6).

———★ ★ ★———

Laced throughout the Word of God, you see the evidence of two things:

- He has expectations for man, declaring that man would be an ever increasing, fruitful, world-dominating being.
- Man has the potential to achieve His expectations because of His power that works in and through us.

Studying these scriptures will reveal key techniques necessary for any All-Star player to achieve ultimate success.

What can I say? That is a wealth of information to absorb.

I am confident you've already began to embrace it all. After all, you were built for this! So, go ahead and take a water break, because we're shifting full speed ahead to the next level.

"Ready?"

"Set?"

"Break!"

CHAPTER 2

Faith to Go the Distance

FAITH FOR THE GOLD

Play #1

★ ★ ★

"BUILT TO LAST"

Congratulations! You've made it through conditioning.

Without a doubt, you are now aware that you have potential faith. Your head is in the game, and you're using mind over matter to show your opponents what you're working with.

There are few who would endure what you did to get here. Then again, not everyone is an All-Star player on this team! Your advantage is great. You've gotten practical insight before stepping into the game.

I sense that you're wondering, "How is that possible?" That is a good question.

Anyone is only as effective as his or her preparation. As stated in the previous chapter, you are being prepared to become an All-Star player with faith for the gold. Our coach [God], doesn't intend for us to get in the game and then give out. He prepares us in every area, guaranteeing that we are built to last. He works to ensure that we have faith that won't quit.

This time around, we're targeting the body. Now, this doesn't mean that you can let your mind roam free. No! Bring your mind in, because you need that too. We're getting ready to activate your faith to go the distance!

In fact, you must have a disciplined mind in order to bring your body into conformity to God's plan. The Apostle Paul was a vigorous player on God's team and his team could count on him to deliver. He understood the importance of keeping his body in subjection to the will of God. That's why he wrote, *"But I keep under my body, and bring it into subjection: lest that by any means, when I have preached to others, I myself should be a castaway"* (1 Corinthians 9:27). As an All-Star player, Paul did not want to be put on the bench to watch others do the hard things or even the seemingly impossible things that God had trained him to do. Can't you see that for yourself? Would you want to go through a demanding training schedule, but then discover that you hadn't brought yourself under the authority of the Head Coach?

If you're wondering, "Why is all this conditioning necessary and when will you be ready to get in the game?" I am prepared to answer those valid questions now.

Many people want to be an overnight wonder. Some people look at you and want to become you overnight, but little do they know that one cannot be a person of great stature and influence that quickly or easily. This is especially true if you are not willing to go the distance. Stop looking at others and thinking you are going to click your heels, stomp your feet, and turn around in the mirror, and hocus pocus, it's going to be done.

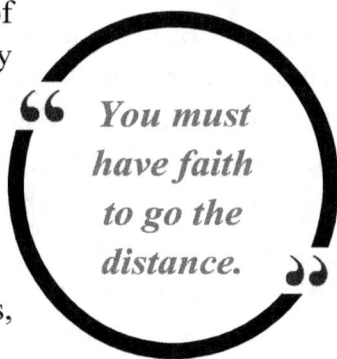

> " *You must have faith to go the distance.* "

You must have faith to go the distance. If it takes fifty years, let it take fifty years. In fact, for Moses, it was 40 years of desert preparation before he was ready to go back to confront Pharaoh. Then, the children of Israel needed another 40 years of wilderness wanderings before they were ready to cross over Jordan and confront their enemies. I guarantee you when you get to the place called promise, God will get the glory, and you will be stronger than ever. I know that the pressure is intense. However, right now you are going to have to rebuke the spirit of surrender and the spirit of shortcut.

Shortcuts are prohibited on God's team. You cannot name it, claim it, and think that it will appear at your doorstep tomorrow.

Until you have faith, and until that faith can go the distance, you're not going to be effective in the All-Star games – you won't be able to execute your responsibilities with maximum potential. When one goes the distance, he or she completes their goal despite all the hardships. They carry out tasks or duties, usually with the connotation that it is arduous in some way. Simply put, faith that goes the distance is a faith that continues until it reaches success. It becomes tough as well as strong. It endures the demands of radical challenges and overcomes.

This part of training is important because many people in the Body of Christ are lazy. That may not be you, but there are lazy Christians out there. They are lazy and get ticked off when they see everyone else getting blessed. They are obviously lacking a faith in them that pushes pass looking blessed and churchy at church, but at home they can't pay their bills. You should not want to look churchy when your car is in jeopardy of being repossessed or your house is about to be foreclosed. The Bible says that He gives us houses that we didn't build and vineyards that we didn't plant. (See Deuteronomy 6:11, Joshua 24:13). God is generous with His team, but He also understands us better than we know ourselves. He doesn't want our faith to be fickle, fragile, faulty, or foolish. Why? Because it reflects badly on Him, as though He hasn't given us all we need to put a big "W" after our names. We are the winners; not the losers. But winners act like winners. They don't sit on the couch claiming victory because their team is winning. NO! They know that they need to be in the game, fighting with all their strength. All their passion, purpose, priority is built on faith that the prize awaits those are aren't distracted by self-indulgence.

Again, the Apostle Paul echoes the thoughts of an Olympic runner when he says, "I press toward the mark for the prize of the high calling of God in Christ Jesus" (Philippians 3:14). He knew he hadn't been called to lie around and take the work of God for granted. He knew that he had to exercise all the faith and all the gifts God had given him in order to receive the victor's crown.

Laziness is not evidence of faith, regardless of how the lazy excuse their failure to act on the truth they've been given. Some people never make the All-Stars because they assume that hard work and faith contradict one another. How stupid! A farmer tills the earth, removing the stones and the weeds, plants good seed, and keeps the pests away. Why does he do all that? Because he knows that the harvest only comes to those who have prepared for it.

Look at faith's hall of fame in Hebrews 11. There we read of the men and women who believed God. They believed God and did great things in His name, not to get faith, but because of the faith God had built into their lives. They had suffered many things, clinging to the promises of the Lord, trusting His Word.

Oh, yes. We read of the glorious things they accomplished.

"Who through faith subdued kingdoms, wrought righteousness, obtained promises, stopped the mouths of lions, Quenched the violence of fire, escaped the edge of the sword, out of weakness were made strong, waxed valiant in fight, turned to fight the armies of the aliens. Women received their dead raised to life again: and others were tortured, not accepting deliverance; that they might obtain a better resurrection..." (Hebrews 11:33-35).

But these heroes of the faith did not have it easy. Many of them suffered terrible abuse and deprivation. Their faith was literally tried in the fire. But they came through shining like gold (See Malachi 3:2-3). Like our Lord, many had those closest to them turn against them. Remember that Job's wife urged him to curse God and die (See Job 2:9). God's All-Star team does not depend on the cheers of the crowd to keep them going. They are not people pleasers.

I submit to you that I am someone who doesn't care about others feelings towards me. No one was there when I spent nights quoting God's Word while all Hell was breaking loose. Therefore, don't get jealous of me, because if you understood the process I went through to get here, then you would understand that the God who blessed me is the God who will bless you. He is no respecter of persons. Therefore, you must be willing to go the distance. It may not happen tomorrow, but toughen up, and suck it up. Stop whining and get a strong back in the Lord.

You will go through some pressure. You will go through perplexity. You will even go through some pitfalls, but you've got a faith that will get you to your promise–even with scars and a couple of bruises.

If you think God has a shortcut for you, you are deceived. Have you ever heard a believer say that Christians won't have to suffer? That's not true! The Bible says that all those who live Godly in Christ Jesus will suffer some persecution (See 2 Timothy 3:12). You've got faith to go through, faith to come out...and when the dust settles you will be standing *with your testimony.*

Any time you do a work for God you will have hardships. However, your ship is harder than the hardship because you have faith to go the distance. This kind of faith is the supernatural power of God made available through man, whereby man can transform conditions, circumstances, and situations in the natural realm. He has been given authority over all these based on the express will of God.

That's what God is doing in your life. He is developing a testimony. You're not just going to testify about life, health, and strength. We all have that! You will have an undeniable, indestructible testimony. *God is getting ready to manifest His glory in your life and the only way God will manifest His glory is if you don't quit now! You've got enough tenacity; you've got enough boldness to go the distance!*

It is imperative that you see yourself as one who has faith to go the distance. You've got the author and the finisher of faith in you (See Hebrews 12:2). You're not just going to start stuff without finishing it. In fact, this is a perfect time to start something. If you have to start by yourself in your basement... making your own website, drawing your own business cards, whatever it is—start now! Not only do you have the faith to start, but you have the grace to finish it.

Make this confession with me. Say, "I'm walking in a finishing grace!"

You are a star performer! Regardless of the problems, perplexities, and persecutions you face, when the dust settles, your faith keeps you standing because faith has enough authority to get things done.

Now if you are in silent contemplation of whether or not your faith can go the distance, do not be dismayed or upset. The fact is that you are right where you need to be.

One's faith cannot go the distance if their faith isn't first made strong. So let's keep building that muscle, shall we?

Play #2

★ ★ ★

"MAN UP"

"Without faith it is impossible to please God. For he that cometh to God must believe that He is…" (Hebrews 11:6).

Stop right there! This is not a game for chumps or the faint of heart. It is so important for you to know that you are built to last through this game. You simply must master how to take your eyes off the problems because they will distract you.

The reason why you can't look at the problem is because looking at it long enough will cause you to give up. All-Stars don't give up, they "man up." This phrase applies to everyone.

You first have to believe in the existence of Jehovah, and that there is no other deity greater than Jesus. After you believe in His existence, you can then believe in His everlasting reward; and that He is a Rewarder to those who go the distance! Confess this aloud. "My faith is getting ready to transform every condition, every circumstance, and every situation."

Three Character Attributes for Having Strong Faith

If one is to be strong in faith, they must walk in three character attributes. They must first walk in consciousness, then consistency, followed by commitment.

Consciousness

Twenty-four hours a day, seven days a week, one must have a God consciousness. This is simply saying that you have to have an awareness of the things of God. You must have a consciousness of where you are going and the promises of God that will get you there.

Consciousness has to be down on the inside of you. You must eat it, drink it, and sleep it until it becomes high definition for you. Do not let the enemy pull you away from seeing it, singing it, praying it, saying it, or writing it, because as you keep on saying, praying, speaking, singing, and writing you will have whatsoever you say! So "whatchu" say?

Consistency

If anything, consistency requires the most effort and intentionality. An All-Star has to continually speak life and have a winner's attitude regardless of what is taking place around them. Everyone gets up at their job after a good Sunday service and preaches to everyone that God is good! They say stuff like, "If you give God your lunch money, He will turn your life around."

The anointing from Sunday spills over into your Monday, and you tell the world about Jesus, but then Tuesday comes, and it's not like it used to be. Now, I am not coming against you believing, because you are a believer. I am, however, posing this question: "Are you a disciple?" The difference between a believer and a disciple is consistency.

I know you believe, but the believers don't get the gold; the disciples do. The Jews believed Jesus, but He desired them to go from being believers to become disciples. Jesus said, *"If you continue in my word, then are ye my disciples indeed"* (John 8:31). Are you a disciple or a believer? This is a life-changing question.

Too many players on the team have settled for just being a believer. They have plummeted to a lower level than what is intended for them. The game can be tiring; that's why some players begin operating in low level status. If you're getting tired, remember the Bible says *"do not get weary in well doing for in due season you'll reap if you faint not"* (Galatians 6:9).

Your faith has to wrap around the fact that your "due season" is coming. Every morning you have get up, open your mouth, and confess that your due season is here, even when it is not here yet. You may be weary right now, but that is all right. Confess that it is here like it is already because one day it is going to be here.

God is shifting things now. He wants disciples to be made.

We should be telling the world that God may not come when we want Him to, but you must continue in the Word. Don't continue in the weariness and don't continue in the worry. You must continue in the Word. You continue in the Word by opening your mouth every single day and confessing His Word.

The doctor may have given you a bad prognosis, but His Word says, by His stripes I am healed (See Isaiah 53:5) and that healing is the children's bread (See Matthew 15:26). You may have gotten a bad report from the IRS or your attorney, but according to His Word, you must confess that no weapon formed against you shall prosper and every tongue that rises up against you, God will judge (See Isaiah 54:17). Confess that the Lord will be with you always, to the four corners of the earth (See Matthew 28:20). You confess that the Lord will supply all of your needs according to His riches in glory (See Philippians 4:19). Therefore, you must continue in the Word.

You can't wait for Monday. You have to do it every day of the week. You have to get yourself in the Word of God every chance you get. You don't have time to be listening to all that jazz music as you call it. You don't have time to watch all that television.

If the truth be told, you know you need too much from the Lord to be in a state of chill. There is nothing wrong with music and other extracurricular activities, but do you have time for that? There is, for example, nothing wrong with taking a vacation, but wait until you get some real money, then you'll be able to really live it up. Let people talk about you. Let them say that you're a party pooper and that you're not really doing anything. I guarantee you that when God gets finished with you, the same people who talked about you will need you.

All-Stars must have the same attitude that Jesus did. You must walk in consistency. I encourage you to stay the course and ride it out. As you walk in consistency, know that evolution is a gradual change. The change may be too slow for you to notice, but it is on God's perfect schedule so that you'll be ready for the championship.

What do you do when unexpected trouble hits your life? Think before you respond. Don't give the church response of hallelujah anyhow, because the truth of the matter is, you know that you bug out and go all crazy. At this point you are going to have a winner's attitude and say Father, *"...though you slay me, yet will I trust You."* (Job 13:15) I'm going to wait until my change comes and while I am waiting I am going to extend my hands and give God the praise, glory, and honor (See Job 13:15).

We are all consistent one way or the other. For instance, you must have a Coke every night before you go to bed. It's not that we don't know the art of consistency, but we use it the wrong way. What if we were to become consistent and driven by our purpose and potential as opposed to our negative proclivities and horrible temperaments? When you get frustrated or your feelings are hurt, you consistently revert to your comfort zones: the big tubs of ice cream, the Lifetime movies, the shades drawn down – moping. We all have consistencies, but we need to operate more in the good ones.

The Bible says that He will keep me in perfect peace if my mind is stayed on Him (See Isaiah 26:3). The Bible tells us to think on those things which are lovely (See Philippians 4:8). Continue in the Word and be consistent, regardless of negative emotions, hurts, and bad feelings. You are not the only person who has been hurt, misused, or abused.

Everyone has. Take a number and we will get to you. Right now, we're on 5,822,543,687,200.

Now let's head back to the subject at hand. When the Coach gets through with you, you will be an MVP, but you must continue through the process. You won't get it if you allow your emotions to get the best of you. You won't get it if you flake out. You are built for this. You are shifting from believer to disciple. The believer has the theory, but not practice. They have the art, but lack the science. Believers have the methods without the mechanics. They have the information, minus implementation.

Consider the person who "believes" that marriage is honorable, yet they still cheat. You can believe something and do the complete opposite.

33

Right now, you believe everything that you are being taught through this book is right, but you still do the opposite. You believe tithing works, but you still don't tithe. You believe that having sex with multiple people could lead to some type of disease, yet you still partake in it. You believe that soul ties are real and whoever you allow into your space will form a soul tie, yet you still allow people to tie into your soul. You are an All-Star player, and you have been commissioned by the Coach to "do." Believing and doing are not synonymous. John 8:31 says, *"If you continue in my word, then are you my disciples."*

Believing and professing you will have a multi-million dollar company is good, but you can't read well. Believing and professing that God is going to put light on your business for all the world to see, but your appearance is sloppy, you need dental work, and you can't speak properly. Why would God do those things, when you are not ready? Faith without works is dead (See James 2:14-26).

> **Whatever you're expecting, you must attach works to it.**

Whatever you're expecting, you must attach works to it. If not, you are going to be like everyone else around you who dreams with no manifested results. You might not be there yet, but continue in the Word of God until you see what you say. Do not give up. Work toward it every day, and you will not fall short of it. Work because you believe God is faithful to reward those who are obedient to His will. That's living faith for you, not that dead stuff that keeps so-called believers on the sofa watching more television than saturating their minds with God's truth.

Evolution is a gradual change. It is not overnight. Many believers are fading away. Paul encourages us to be not weary in well doing because in due season we will reap if we faint not (See Galatians 6:9).

Don't get tired of living holy. It is not easy because you live in a world that is not holy. Sometimes, it seems like you are swimming upstream against the current because the whole world is pushing you away from your goal. That's when you need a strength that just isn't there for those who praise God on Sunday but sing a different tune the rest of the week.

Jesus says "I know that you have to live within this world that is not holy, so I am going to give you the Holy Ghost. I have to put something in you so that you can remain holy in an unholy world. You need more than Casper the friendly ghost. You need more than goosebumps. You need more than a chill and a thrill. You need the indwelling power of the Holy Ghost that keeps you consistent, committed, and holy. When you really get the Holy Ghost, you will get a weight and consistency in your spirit.

My wife and I have been married for over eighteen years now, and we are still continuing. There were no successful marriages in my family. They had babies out of wedlock. I was a bastard. I was illegitimate, but I am the most anointed bastard most of you will ever see. The importance of me saying this is because you have to be aware of the generational curses you fight. Be aware of your blessings, but also know what it is that you have to fight. It is as simple as knowing your friends and your enemies.

You need to know who is on the same team with you and those who aren't. You need to know how the curses that have robbed, ruined, and ruptured the lives of your family need not descend upon you and yours. Jesus became a curse for you so that you could become a blessing for others (See Galatians 3:13; 1 Peter 3:9; Zechariah 8:13).

I shared earlier that my wife and I have been married for a while now, and I have been continuing in my love walk with her.

There was a time I was frustrated with her. I wanted to leave, get in the car and never come back. In that time, the Lord spoke to me and said, "If you take care of Stephanie, I will take care of you." Now, I am not like phony Christians. If God tells me something, I am sold on it even when my flesh says otherwise. From that time, it has become my highest joy to manifest every desire that my wife has. I want her to have memories that make her say, "There was nothing I wanted, that he didn't promptly make happen for me."

At this point of the work out, you have to take your religious glasses off. Now, put them on the floor and stomp on them. Stephanie had never been to California, specifically, Rodeo Drive, but it was her desire to go. She used her faith. The same faith that got you saved is the same faith that can make your dreams a reality.

Stephanie started confessing aloud that she would walk the streets of "*Pretty Woman*." She kept saying that she would visit the same stores that Julia Roberts did in "*Pretty Woman*." After preaching multiple services, I told her to pack a bag for 48 hours because I wanted to take her somewhere. We got on the plane and right before takeoff, the attendant announced on the speaker that our next stop was LAX! Stephanie got excited, and rightfully so. She knew she had just come from confessing this. Now faith is the substance of things hoped for, it's the evidence

36

of things not seen (See Hebrews 11:1). *"Without faith, it is impossible to please God for he that cometh to God must believe that He is and that He is a rewarder to them that diligently seek him"* (Hebrews 11:6). On our way back from the trip, she said that her entire belief shifted.

Another description of hope is *expecting*. So, faith is the substance of what I am hoping for. Take for instance this scenario. You've been running all day. Just as with this spiritual workout, you have been working out in the natural. At the end of the workout, you are expecting to have some type of hydration–a bottle of water. Faith must wrap around what I am expecting in order to bring it to me.

If that was not a clear enough example, consider this one.

You are single, and you are tired of sleeping by yourself. You made up in your mind that you are not going to sleep around. You are not going to lose your anointing by fornicating. You desire someone with whom you will spend the rest of your life. Therefore, you set your expectations on a spouse. You are not going to get that spouse unless you attach your faith to that expectation.

Faith pulls your expectation closer to you.

The reason faith gets expectation closer to you is because you make faith confessions. Every day you get up you say, "Lord, I thank You for my Abigail (single man confession) or my Abraham (single female confession). I thank You for a spouse that loves You and loves me. I thank You for a spouse that reverences You. I thank You for a spouse that helps to build up our house. I thank You for an intercessor and a prayer warrior. Lord, I thank You for not giving me a spouse that is Jezebel, stupid, fat, ugly, and slow. Thank You for a fine spouse, a beautiful spouse, a spouse who, when others see them, they want them too."

Every time you open your mouth and start confessing, confessions wrap around your expectation and brings it into existence. If your expectation is not connected to faith, it is dead hope (See James 2:17), and hope delayed makes the heart sick (See Proverbs 13:12). Have you ever had delayed hope? When you look back over our life, you can see the areas where you did not connect your faith to what you were expecting. We have all been guilty of this.

The confusion comes when you believe that hope is faith. Hope is not faith. Faith means I am one hundred percent assured that whatever He said, He has already brought it to pass. Whatever I am expecting, I must call my faith into connection with it. Keep trusting. Keep hoping. Keep believing.

Without faith, you would not be able to see God's provision even if He put it right in front of you. Some idiots talk about "blind faith." Excuse me, but faith is a revelation that lets you see what God is doing even when the flesh cannot.

I believe God wants you to live a fabulous life. When Stephanie and I were confessing this, we were still living in an apartment, and she was wearing 'hand-me-down' thrift store suits. We never let our present hinder our future.

God put you here, so you need to stay in position until increase hits your life. Every time you are being stretched to the next level, that's when you try to run away. You are a runner. However, you have been planted here; and because of that, you are getting ready to flourish here. Get ready for dynamic testimonies. Get ready for an extraordinary move of the Spirit of God in your house.

This is why you have to get up every day and say, *"This is the day that the Lord has made. I will rejoice and be glad in it"* (Psalm 118:24). Yes, I know you've said it already, but say it again. Confess that you are the head and not the tail, that you shall lend and not borrow, that you are above and not beneath, that you are blessed in the city and blessed in the field, blessed when you come and blessed when you go (See Deuteronomy 15:6, 28:2-13). Confess that you are blessed and your family is blessed. Confess that you will never be broke, not another day in your life. Confess that the blood of Jesus covers you and no sickness will penetrate through it. Confess that this day will be the start of the best days of your life. Continue saying this aloud until you see it before you.

Commitment

With all the previous information about consistency, I'm certain you have forgotten that there us yet still another attribute left to discuss, and that is commitment. This is the part of the walk where you will be required to commit to the previous two.

Whatever you say contrary to the will and Word of God while making your way forward in the game can forfeit the progress you've already made. For example, for the last 29 days, you have been saying you will never be broke another day in your life. Then, on the 30th day, you open your mouth and say, "Is this ever going to change for me? This must just be my plight in life." You have just delayed your progress and denied the confessions of the past 29 days. Now you will have to get out of the line and go back to the starting point.

It does get hard at times. As you keep playing for God, your opponent the devil will work to tempt you and try to convince you that it cannot be done. His tactics can make you feel like forfeiting, tapping out. Nevertheless, you must profess the truth that the devil is a liar (See John 8:44). When you feel like throwing in the towel, you must command your hand to hold on to that towel. Commit to the game and your position on the team by reminding yourself and the devil that, whatever God starts, He is big enough to complete it. He that begun a good work in you and is able to complete it (See Philippians 1:6). Stay the course!

The Word is your course – your game plan. It shows destination. The course has already been designed. God does not need you as a co-architect or co-assistant to help in the development of the course. The course was designed before you were in the earth.

For I know the course. The course is to bless you and give you a future and bring you to and expected end (See Jeremiah 29:11).

You must watch what you say while on the course. You should not confess things like, "I'm sick as a dog" "You are gonna' make me lose my mind" "I am serious as a heart attack" because life and death are in the power of your tongue. This is why you are to get up and confess, *"This is the day that the Lord has made, I will rejoice and be glad in it"* (Psalm 128:24). "I am the head and not the tail. I am a lender and not a borrower. I am above and not beneath" (See Deuteronomy 28:13).

This course is not a one hundred-yard dash. You must continue in it. It is not a sprint. Back in the day, and even now, whatever God gave me, I honored it. I kept my apartment clean, and our little "hooptie" was washed. Every time I washed our Maxima, I confessed that it was a Mercedes. I wrapped my faith around my expectation, and today I own that Mercedes, along with two others. God can do the same thing for you. While you are being blessed, keep in mind that the blessings aren't given so that the saints know you are blessed. You haven't arrived until sinners know who you are. You don't have to make Jesus famous at church, make him famous in the marketplace.

You must be committed to stay the course all the way to the end of the race (See 2 Timothy 4:7).

Play #3

★ ★ ★

"HE'S GOT GAME"

If your faith muscle wasn't strong before, I know it is gaining strength now. It has no choice but to get stronger with all this lean Word it's enduring. Because we've built your faith muscles to last, let's see what kind of game you've got when you put it to work.

Start working your oil and stop giving it freely. You are a star performer on this team. Don't play yourself cheap. The world needs to pay millions for your oil. *Your oil will not only bless others, but it will get you out of debt.*

Put your oil to work before someone steals it because oil stealers do exist.

These people come in while you're asleep and take your idea, concept, and work. However, the devil is a liar. You paid a price for the oil you have. You've been through Hell and back, just to tell God 'Thank you!' So, work it!

The Oil Flow from Your Faith

A successful oil flow will come from the consistent intensity of your faith flow. Throughout the Bible God shows his players that the use of faith is favorable in the All-Star games.

When you play the game in faith, the coach will inevitably do certain things. God will respect it! God will respond to it! God will reward it!

Respect

God respected Abel's faith. In the book of Genesis, you find that because of man's sin, God cursed the earth; meaning that He cursed the ground.

The Bible tells us that Abel had such great faith that when Cain gave God anything, Abel gave God a more perfect sacrifice. Abel offered God sheep. Something with a heartbeat. Cain gave God something that he got from the ground. God says, *"He doesn't want any more cursed offerings. He wants an offering that is alive and has a heartbeat."*

Understand this, in this game, you have to be very careful that you don't show up to the game looking like a mannequin or like a corpse. When you come to the game, you are presenting your body as a living sacrifice, holy and acceptable. God wants a heartbeat. He wants something He can feel. Give God something that He can feel. Make sure your love is for real!

Respond

As I mentioned previously, God responds to faith. When you use your faith, God responds to it. Take Noah for example. Noah was building an ark for one hundred and twenty years, and God responded to his faith.

> *...God responds to FAITH.*

God responded to Noah's faith when He made it rain.

It may not look like it or seem like it, but God is going to respond to the faith you express. Don't act on what you see

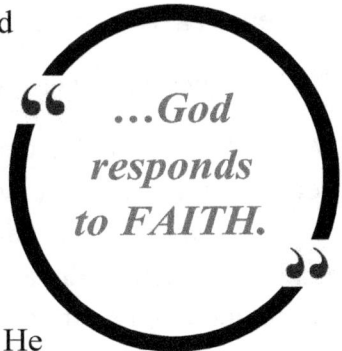

43

because looks can be deceiving. "We look not at the things which are seen; for the things which are seen are temporal; and the things which are not seen are eternal" (2 Corinthians 4:18).

Reward

Now let's consider the third action of God. God will reward your faith. The Bible tells us about Abraham and how he had such great faith that he was called the father of faith (See Romans 4:16). God rewarded his faith as righteousness.

Abraham never had on a long dress. He never went to church on Sunday. He never took communion on first Sunday. He never had a veil and never had a clergy shirt; but because he had such great faith, God told him, "You're righteous."

This is the point you must reach. Nothing, and no one can compare to your God. Whatever God says, God does. Whatever God wants, God gets.

If those weren't enough to keep you motivated, let me share with you my personal testimony on how these three truths were evident in my All-Star training process.

"When I was poor...yes, you read correctly."

When I was poor and living in an apartment, I was sitting reading, and Stephanie was somewhere doing whatever she was doing. God had me to read Psalms 112:3; and in that moment I said to myself, "Her family is broke! My family is broke! But we're not about to stay broke!"

Now I was not complaining, because I know if I complain I'll remain. My wife however, was a new babe in the Lord, so she complained, whined, and cried. She asked, why can't we go here? Why can't I wear that? She complained so much that I had to encourage her. I told her that a day would come where she will no longer have a complaint about those things.

Do not get me wrong. Telling Stephanie not to complain and that things wouldn't always be like this was good, but that was not what brought change in our lives. Just speaking it would be wishful thinking. I had to find something in the Word. I had to find the promises of God.

This was particularly hard for me because I came from a church that told me that the saints did not need to be rich; instead, we only needed Jesus. I had Stephanie get her Bible, and we opened it to Psalms 112:3. When I saw that God said "wealth and riches shall be in my house;" I knew that every "shall" in the Word of God is loaded with dynamite. My faith was so stirred that I began declaring Psalms 112:3 throughout the house. I looked at our mattress that was on the floor on top of the box spring, and I said, "Replace!" It had to be replaced because when you slept on it, you had to do so at an angle or else the springs would stick you. Stephanie was looking at me like I was crazy at that point. I looked at my old leaky refrigerator that was leaking that old brown sludge that we had to clean up every thirty days and said, "Replace!"

After that I turned to Job 36:11, and it read, *"They that serve him will spend their days in prosperity and their years in pleasures."* I want you to know that sanctimonious people will attempt to box you in by telling you not to pray for money.

However, the Word of God tells us that we have not because we ask not (See James 4:3). It further states that money answers all things (See Ecclesiastes 10:19). When you find a promise in the Word of God, you must open your mouth and declare it.

I began to think about the bounced checks I had written, and immediately began putting the blame on God. The church I came from told me that God does everything. They told me if God wants you to have a better job, He'll give you a better one. I spent a lot of my life blaming God for everything. He showed me that He was not the one bouncing the checks; I was. He showed me that my faith was dead. The reason why my apartment was ugly, why checks were bouncing, why my ends weren't meeting, and why I had anxiety attacks when the first of the month came around was because I needed my faith to be resurrected. God was taking this opportunity to develop me into an All-Star player. I had to open my mouth and begin confessing Job 36:11 over my life and my home.

As I continued in the Word, God showed me Job 22:27. Through this scripture, God told me that if I want something from Him, I have to invest a seed with it. The scripture says, "You shall make your prayer unto Him and He shall hear thee and thou shall pay thy vows, then you can decree a thing." By that point, I had gotten bold. I told God that I had been praying. Once those words had left my lips, my spirit was provoked to get a seed in my hand. I began confessing Psalms 112:3, Job 36:11, and Job 22:27. It wasn't easy though, because I started to think about all the bills due and all the people I owed. I just knew God was trying to take what I had.

That was my problem. I failed to realize that God was not trying to take anything from me, He was trying to get something to me. I had to change the way I saw the promises of God so that I could see them manifest in my life.

I had to come against stinking thinking and command my mind to be washed by the Word of God so that I could see God at His best! At that time, all I had was ten dollars. I took that money to church, put it on the altar, and told God that it was all I had, but I am sowing it to put action to the Word. Even now, I prophetically decree and declare that you will see God's healing, deliverance, and freeing power in your life, in Jesus' name.

As an All-Star, you are going to have to put the work in, just as I did. None of us are exempt from the process. Whatever you need to believe God for, whether it is healing, deliverance, or breakthrough, find those promises in the Word of God and confess them over your life daily. Simply sitting there and not doing anything, is going to produce exactly that-not a thing!

Faith is a necessary arsenal for players in this game. When the believer is standing in faith for something they have seen in the Word of God, they must have five justifiable expectations. God will give you a plan of action, the wisdom of God, the favor of God, a miracle, and strength to endure until you see change.

> " *Faith is a necessary arsenal for players in this game.* "

Five Justifiable Expectations of the Believer

Plan of Action – A plan is needed because faith without works is dead. It is merely wishful thinking to believe God for millions when you don't get up to work for it. As an All-Star on this team, you do not sit there and wait for your ship to come in. You have the authority to jump in the ocean and pull your ship to you.

Wisdom of God – Since your vision is God's idea, you need His wisdom. Without the wisdom of God, you will lose what you get just as fast as you get it. Many people have lost more without wisdom than they have gained with wisdom. Wisdom is about understanding and prioritizing. If you get an extra thousand dollars this week, you don't go off and spend it. You pay your tithes and give an offering, and then save the rest. That money is not really extra. It could be part of God's provision for something you don't see yet.

Favor of God – After the plan of God is set in place, and the wisdom of God has been downloaded, the favor of God comes into play. The favor of God is revealed when God raises up someone to use their power, ability, and influence to help you. You remember the story I previously shared, right? Well, when I began believing God for new furniture, He released His favor towards me. Someone knocked on my door and shared that he had noticed my family and me having church in the house. He shared that he and his wife were getting a divorce. He had just bought brand new furniture, which he got in the divorce and did not want. Making a long story short, he said if you want it and can come get it from the warehouse it's in, it is yours. That is the favor of God. He raised up someone to help me.

A Miracle – If God does not give you a plan of action, His wisdom, or His favor, then He will most definitely give you a miracle. The miracle of God is simply this: you do not know how it is going to happen, but all of a sudden God steps in and makes a way.

Strength to Endure – Through all of this, you must have strength to endure until you see change. You must be assured that no matter how much is going on around you, when the dust settles, your faith will have kept you standing.

Most All-Star players dislike that last step. It's a time of standing still. Control is no longer yours, but belongs only to the coach. This is when you have no choice but to wait until you are directed to make your next move.

The Believer's Water Break

God is very much aware of this process. This is why amidst the games, He gives us a water break. It's in this time that we must **R.E.S.T!**

Renew – You must know and believe that your current condition is not your concrete conclusion. You will never really see God's glory in the midst of hell until you first renew your mind." *And be not conformed to this world: but be ye transformed by the renewing of your mind, that ye may prove what is that good, and acceptable, and perfect, will of God"* (Romans 12:2).

Endure – What you are going through is a temporary condition, knowing it only lasts for a little while. It is natural not to believe this. You more than likely don't believe it is a temporary condition because you have been going through it for years. The truth is that you have been going through it as long as you have because you are saying and thinking the wrong stuff. You will come out of the situation based on your thinking process and your communication level. You have to know it won't last, so don't give it any more attention. "Beloved, think it not strange concerning the fiery trial which is to try you, as though some strange thing happened unto you: But rejoice, inasmuch as ye are partakers of Christ's sufferings; that, when his glory shall be revealed, ye may be glad also with exceeding joy" (1 Peter 4:12-13). When fiery trials come–and they will–it is time to chill out.

Stand – Hold fast to God's Word until the promise manifests! Do not sway on the Word, plant your feet firmly on it. "He staggered not at the promises of God through unbelief; but was strong in faith, giving glory to God; and being fully persuaded that, what he had promised, he was able also to perform" (Romans 4:20-21). You must be fully persuaded and fully convinced of what God's Word says. Be so much convinced that if you died in this moment you have to come back to life because you have not seen or laid hold of all God has promised you.

Trust – Believe God for the results because He is your deliverer. Let go of being the perfectionist. Let go of doing it yourself. The curse of independence is that you are so independent that you are void of faith. You be you and allow God to be God. The truth is you are a worrier. You have to work twenty-five times harder to make sure that something is done. This is not you working in faith; this is you working in anxiety. Look at Martha in the book of Luke. She was cumbered about much serving (See Luke 10:40). Working in anxiety causes you to break out on your face or gain weight. You can't have faith and worry at the same time. You are going to have to trust the process. You don't need to know how God is going to do it.

Your role in the process is to go to bed and keep getting up and confessing. Don't worry, God will speak to the earth, the man, or the problem, and it must give up the harvest. You have to trust that God will manifest the results.

And he said, so is the kingdom of God, as if man should cast seed into the ground; and should sleep, and rise night and day, and the seed should spring and grow up, he noweth not how. For the earth bringeth forth fruit of herself; first the blade, then the ear, after that the full corn in the ear. But when the fruit is brought forth, immediately he putteth in the sickle, because the harvest is come (Mark 4:26-29).

In Romans, Abraham staggered not at the promises of God through unbelief but was strong in faith giving glory to God. To stagger means to walk or move unsteadily as if you are about to fall. Stop wobbling! No more walking unsteady and shakily.

You are an All-Star player. You walk by faith and not by sight (See 2 Corinthians 5:7). If you want to get the gold, you must continue in the word because faith comes by hearing and hearing by the Word of God (See Romans 10:17).

The Word is your compass. It shows the direction you should go. David said this in Psalms 119:5, "The word is a lamp unto my feet and a light unto my path." Use the compass you were given. Get out of everyone's face and get into the Word.

When pressure, perplexity, and persecution comes you cannot stagger at the promises of God. The Word gives direction for every area of life, whether it is health, finances, marriage, business, or whatever else. You must let the devil know that you know that the promise is on its way. Persecution is only an indicator that breakthrough is around the corner.

The Word of God is constructive; it shows development. Only the Word can develop you into a champion. *"Now brethren, I commend you to God and to the word of His grace, which is able to build you up and give you an inheritance among those that are sanctified"* (Acts 20:32). It is evident that the Word builds you and then gives you an inheritance. You will never walk into your overflow until you get in the Word. You will also never walk into overflow until the Word has built you up.

The things the enemy has tried to scare you and intimidate you with, because you have been in the Word, God said you have been built up in some areas so now the devil must flee. Things that once bothered you will no longer bother you. Things that made you angry, no longer make you angry. The things that depressed you, will no longer depress you because you are in the Word of God, and you know that all things work together for your good (See Romans 8:28).

Some things are about to hit the body of Christ. A shift is coming to the body of Christ that has been sold out to the things of God. They are calling those things that are not as though they were. They are not speaking into their present, but they are speaking into their future. They are dragging their future into their present, and their present is turning into their dream.

Your season of more than enough, your season of promise is upon you like never before, and God is raising up someone, somewhere to use their power, influence, and ability to help you. Help is on the way, help for your business, ministry, family, and your marriage.

With all the stuff you dream of doing, you know you need some help. You are not dreaming of a mom and pop chain. You are dreaming of a vast enterprise. Wealth and riches should be in our house. The world is supposed to see our riches and be awed. Let your light so shine before men that they may see your good works, and glorify God (See Matthew 5:16). That is what God is working out with you. He is working to put 'works' under your belt.

You have a choice. You don't have to be here. You can stop right here and turn back. You are only losing time, energy, and effort, right? Determine how important those are to you. The choice is yours. You don't have to be on the team. However, if you want to be here, get in the game, and stop watching from the sidelines. You have what it takes. You've got game.

Play #4

★ ★ ★

"NO 'I' IN TEAM"

This is amazing! From mind to body, you're well on your way to being whole in your faith. You aren't the only person who has gone through this process. You are joining the MVPs who have played this game too. Biblically, Joseph, Job, and Jesus are three of many players who have been where you are today.

Joseph withstood the process of training for many years (See Genesis 37:2, 41:46). It took thirteen years from the prophecy to the manifestation. Job, through his training lost all substance and sources. His own wife turned on him. Jesus the Christ is the ultimate All-Star.

Through His training, He came through 42 generations, being born of a virgin. He grew up in Nazareth and started His ministry. He was hated by both the religious and political parties. He endured being beaten by members of these parties. They placed a crown of thorns on His head. Jesus then died, but got back up in three days with all power!

These three men, if anything, show us that endurance through the process of faith-building pays off in ways greater than can be imagined. Considering the processes of Joseph, Job, and Jesus can be a bit intimidating, so consider the following contemporary examples. They too have endured processes of intense training.

Gabrielle Douglas is first in the lineup. This young African American girl represented her country at the 2012 Summer Olympics in London. Undergoing countless practices, Gabrielle was able to overcome the odds by walking away with gold medals in both the team and individual all-around competitions. Not only is she a national champion, she is the first woman of color of any nationality to become the Individual All-Around Champion. Gabrielle is also the first American to win gold in both gymnastic competitions at the same Olympic Games.

Another great contemporary example is the Williams sisters: Venus and Serena. These two women are professional American tennis players. Undergoing intense coaching from their parents, Richard Williams and Oracene Price, both Venus and Serena Williams were able to achieve singles "Grand Slam" title status. They even competed in tournaments against each other. Two of their popular rivalry games were the 2001 U.S Open and the 2009 Wimbledon Tournament. Their competitiveness stays on the court as each of them lends support to the other by watching the games even if they have been knocked out of the competition.

Those two snapshots are good, but there's yet still another; the one and only Michael Phelps. Born in June of 1985 in Baltimore Maryland, Michael attests to having undergone countless, intense training sessions. His willingness to endure the process of training prepared him to compete in his first Olympic Game with the U.S men's swim team at age 15. Since that initial competition, Michael has gone on to win medals in the Athens, Beijing, London, and Rio Olympics. Even with his brief retirement, he is currently the most decorated Olympian in history. He has a total of 28 medals, with 23 of those being gold.

Along with his ability to win, he is also a well-known record setter.

There you have it! You are not in this by yourself. There is nothing you are enduring in this process that hasn't been endured by others who have gone before you or who play beside you. Like Gabby Douglas, you've competed solo, like the Williams sisters, you sit out and cheer others on. Like Michael Phelps, you may even choose to sit out for a season or two, but the love of the game is still very much alive and in you. You were born to go for the gold.

> *" You were born to go for the gold. "*

***

I don't think you realize it, but you are a force to be reckoned with! You have covered a lot of ground, and that is not to be taken lightly. A pat on the back and a lifting of the head is due.

Now, don't get too comfortable here. There is still more to cover. So, go ahead and stretch those limbs, and take a swig of water because it only intensifies from here.

"Ready?"

"Set?"

"Break!"

CHAPTER 3

The Saga

FAITH FOR THE GOLD

Play #1

"HIGH LEVEL INTENSITY TRAINING"

Congratulations! Those words seem quite fitting. You are making great progress. Coach did right when He drafted you for this team.

Your potential faith is in effect. I can tell your head is in the game, and you're using mind over matter to show your opponents what they are up against. Without a doubt, your faith to go the distance is engaged. You have manned up because you understand that you're not alone on this team. Like many who have gone before you, you're built to last, and like them, you've got game.

Now just as in the trainings before, we need your mind and your body present and accounted for. With both working in their respective capacities, you'll be able to endure this high-level intensity training!

***

Let's look closely at a veteran player for our team, Job. He was a champion before our days. However, he is our coach's number one pick to prepare you for the high-level intensity of the game. High-level intensity training comes when you must use faith amidst darkness, distress, and disaster.

The book of Job has 1,070 verses totalling 10,102 words. It is the 18th book of the Bible and the first of the five poetic books.

Job's name is said to have two possible meanings. Job in Hebrew means "the persecuted one," and in Arabic means, "repentant one."

Job was a man of great wealth and stature before his unfortunate series of events [saga]. Just like you, he was drafted onto the All-Star team. He underwent rigorous training just as you are now undergoing.

> **God uses trials and tribulations to shape our character…**

Job and God worked together for years. This is why he was able to acquire all the spiritual depth and vigorous faith that he had.

Without God, Job wouldn't have achieved all he did. He didn't achieve his wealth and success without persevering through intense situations where he felt alone. That is true for all of us. Jesus made it very plain when He said, *"…without me ye can do nothing"* (John 15:5). Of course, that doesn't mean we can't mess things up without God's help. He isn't the cause of our failures, but He does use them as the raw material to shape us. We cannot accomplish anything of significance without God's enabling power in the midst of it.

God uses trials and tribulations to shape our character and strengthen our faith. Like a refiner of precious metals, He uses the heat of the furnace to remove the dross of impurities. When He's finished, He brings those troubles to an end, and we are ready for the gold.

During those times, we may feel like God has vanished from the scene, like He is unaware of our struggles and pain, but even when we cannot see Him at work, He is watching us. He is preparing us for the championship.

"On the left hand, where he doth work, but I cannot behold him: he hideth himself on the right hand, that I cannot see him: But he knoweth the way that I take: when he hath tried me, I shall come forth as gold" (Job 23:9).

I'm certain that you're familiar with his story, but in the event that you're not, the snapshot account of his life is that Job was a man of great wealth, stature, and spirit. He had land, luxury, and legacy. Within a matter of hours, Job's profound life was turned to tumult when he lost all his children, livestock, and home. His body was stricken with boils, and he had no help or compassion from his wife or friends.

Job struggled under the burden of his infirmities and afflictions. He couldn't understand the meaning of God's providence concerning him. He went forward, but it seemed like God wasn't there to hear his case. He went back, but it seemed he couldn't find God anywhere. He went left and he went right, and to no avail. He came up empty.

Although Job knew that God was ever-present, it seems that he was unable to form a clear conception of things in his mind. He became so confused, so strained with his troubles, that he became a man at his wit's end.

Confusion clears up nothing. Job was at a loss, trying to know what God had purposed to do with him. When Job was called into the game, he had to put the chaos aside and to demonstrate what God had given to him. It wasn't easy. The intensity of the game caused his faith to falter a bit, but it didn't fumble. Faith that won't fumble is a faith that will go the distance. Whether under trial, test, or turbulence, it comes through it all triumphantly!

In any earthly sport, the victories that matter for the championship don't come without effort and hardship.

Play #2

★ ★ ★

"WINNING WITH WHAT YOU'VE GOT"

Remember that faith is the supernatural power of God made available through man, whereby man can transform conditions, circumstances, and situations in the natural realm over which he has been given authority, based on the express will of God.

It wasn't just good enough that Job knew what to do. He had to do what he knew. In order for his conditions to change, Job had to play the hand he was dealt as opposed to complaining about the hand he had. If you complain, you will remain and *ain't* nobody got time for that!

Remember, when Coach puts you in the game, He does it with the confidence that you won't give up or give out. You are built to last! You have faith that continues until it reaches success. Although Job didn't know which way to go, his contentment remained. The steadfastness of his faith continued. God witnessed Job's integrity. Throughout his high-level intensity training, Job believed that God knew which way he should take, and that whatever the way was, it was good.

Sometimes, we don't have a perfect understanding of God's will in a situation. Until he shows you what to do, you must rest up and get ready for your assignment. You must have the confidence that He knows what's best and knows exactly when to reveal where you fit into His supernatural game plan. Unless you have faith, you won't be able to rest. You'll exhaust your energy fretting about things you don't know because you don't need to know them.

Like many other areas of life, our success can be based on Who we know more than what we know. Because we have such confidence in our Coach, we can relax and enjoy the journey as we get ready for the next play. Once you do know what God wants, get with it! Don't complain about the assignment being too tough. Don't whine and ask "Why me?" Don't compare your difficulties with the easy life that others seem to be enjoying.

***

With the understanding of faith and what it is for, you too must do what you know. Play the hand you were dealt.

What is going on around you? What have you lost?

How many family and friends have stood against you? You too have a hand that you were dealt. Use that hand, your potential faith, and your faith to go the distance to overcome the high level of intensity you're up against. With those strategies in place, you cannot lose.

Maybe you are struggling with the loss of a job, with kids who break your heart, with sickness that limits your strength and causes pain. Whatever the obstacles, you are designed to overcome them.

Once you've completed the training we've been discussing, you must not second guess Coach when He sends you into the critical play of the game. It isn't time to throw up your hands and quit. Great challenges like you are facing are the defining moments that will shape your future for years to come.

These techniques can even be coupled with the following faith conditioning scriptures. These are perfect when you're in the dark, distress, or in the midst of delivery.

All-Star Faith Conditioning Scriptures

Faith in the Dark

"For we walk by faith, not by sight" (2 Corinthians 5:7).

* * *

"For we walk by faith [we regulate our lives and conduct ourselves by our conviction or belief respecting man's relationship to God and divine things, with trust and holy fervor; thus we walk] not by sight or appearance" (2 Corinthians 5:7 AMP).

* * *

"This poor man cried, and the LORD heard him, and saved him out of all his troubles" (Psalm 34:6).

Faith in Distress

"Fear thou not; for I am with thee: be not dismayed; for I am thy God: I will strengthen thee; yea, I will help thee; yea, I will uphold thee with the right" (Isaiah 41:10).

* * *

"The LORD also will be a refuge for the oppressed, a refuge in times of trouble" (Psalm 9:9).

* * *

"God is our refuge and strength, a very present help in trouble" (Psalm 46:1).

Be careful for nothing; but in everything by prayer and supplication with thanksgiving let your requests be made known unto God. And the, which passeth all understanding, shall keep your hearts and minds through Christ Jesus. Finally, brethren, whatsoever things are true, whatsoever things are honest, whatsoever things are just, whatsoever things are pure, whatsoever things are lovely, whatsoever things are of good report; if there be any virtue, and if there be any praise, think on these things (Philippians 4:6-8).

* * *

There hath no temptation taken you but such as is common to man: but God is faithful, who will not suffer you to be tempted above that ye are able; but will with the temptation also make a way to escape, that ye may be able to bear it (1 Corinthians 10:13).

* * *

Casting all your care upon him; for he careth for you (1 Peter 5:7).

* * *

Yea, and all that will live godly in Christ Jesus shall suffer persecution (2 Timothy 3:12).

* * *

Casting the [a] whole of your care] all anxieties, all your worries, all your concerns, [b]once and for all] on Him, for He cares for you affectionately and cares about you[c] watchfully (1 Peter 5:7 AMP).

Faith in Delivery

For whatsoever is born of God overcometh the world: and this is the victory that overcometh the world, even our faith (1 John 5:4)

---- * * * ----

The angel of the LORD encampeth round about them that fear him, and delivereth them. O taste and see that the LORD is good: blessed is the man that trusteth in him. O fear the LORD, ye his saints: for there is no want to them that fear him (Psalm 34:7-9).

Understand that we must be led by conviction, which is a fixed or firmly held belief. All-Stars must also be led by commitment, which is to bind and obligate. Lastly, we are to be led by communion, which is our relationship with Christ.

Play #3

★ ★ ★

"PLAY SMARTER NOT HARDER"

With all this training and muscle building, it's easy to grow hard. But, harder is not necessarily smarter.

Job was a man as intense as the game was. He played the game smart, not hard. He understood that although God seemed to be untraceable and unreachable, He wasn't unknowing.

God's thoughts are far above our thoughts. God is God! He is *the* Coach. He is to be extolled, infinitely exalted above all the things here below. God is acquainted with our way. He is on our side when everyone else deserts us. He still knows those marvelous plans He has for you (See Jeremiah 29:11), and He will not change His mind (See Malachi 3:6).

Friends may charge us of things of which we are not guilty. We may experience terrific afflictions and terrible pains, but God has a purpose and a reason for everything we experience. This is Job's assurance and why he could profess in chapter twenty-three, *"He knoweth the way that I take: when he hath tried me, I shall come forth as gold"* (Job 23:10).

The purity of gold is defined either in karats or fineness.

A karat is 1/24 part of pure gold by weight, thus making 24 karat gold, pure gold. For one to find the percentage of gold in an object with its purity stated in karats, they must multiply the number of karats by 100 and then divide the answer by 24.

We're not all mathematicians, I know. So here goes an example.

12 karat gold is 50% pure gold. The equation would look somewhat like this:

$$12 \times 100 \div 24 = 50\%$$

Do you have 24 karat faith? Has your faith been purified in the fires of frustration and apparent failure? Once it is refined, you'll understand it when I tell you that for someone with All-Star faith, no failure is final. Don't quit in the middle of the story! Wait until the "happily ever after part" when God leads you to victory.

How is all of this playing smart and not hard? I'm glad you asked.

Job allowed his assurance to be the governing force of his belief. He was certain that God was in control and that He knew everything taking place. He also chose to confess his assurance aloud to ensure that his surroundings got the news.

Instead of working in his own strength or in the strength of others, he simply allowed God to be God. Job acknowledged that what he was going through was temporary, and he endured with the knowledge that it would all be over soon.

> " With All-Star faith, no failure is final. "

With certainty, Job states that after the moments of pressure are over, he will come forth as pure gold! Gold is refined of its impurities by fire. This means that the pressure and the process [high intensity levels] were only removing the trash – some relationships, friendships, courtships, fellowships, internships that are being burnt away. Know this also, 24 karat gold is the softest and most fine gold there is. God is making us soft in areas where we are hard and calloused.

People often describe Job as incredibly patient, and that is quite true. However, few recognize the source of his patience. It wasn't from the suffering he experienced. When James 1 says that the testing of our faith brings patience, we often miss the point (See James 1:3).

Patience comes from faith being tested. Without testing by difficult circumstances, faith may not seem very strong, but those hard times prove something. The Greek word that is translated "patience" can also be translated "endurance." It implies not giving up when going through a serious challenge.

How much would it take to make you throw in the towel and quit trying? Would you give up if you lost everything and everyone, including your children and your own health? Many people would be so crushed by those blows that they would confess, "Why try? It hurts too much. How could God expect me to go forward after this?"

You might feel like a running back who rushes forward, only to be pushed back over ten yards. You could feel like the basketball center who goes through an entire game without scoring.

How strong in the Lord is your faith? Are you ready for high-level intensity in your life? How will you handle the darkness, distress, and disorder that the devil intends to bring against you? Will you surrender before you see the end game that the Coach has planned?

Get in there with the grit and determination that comes from a faith that is focused by conviction, commitment, and communion. Dwell on the power God has available for you, not the false power of the devil and his team of losers.

***

Oh my goodness, what a workout right? That was intense.

Kudos to you. You've endured the stages of conditioning, muscle building, and training. Again, I say to you, congratulations!

You've been a good student. I sense your muscles are rearing to get a piece of the action. So, I'll tell you what, take a breather, and let's get you ready. We're making our way to the Olympic Games.

"Ready?"

Don't get scared. "Set?"

Remember, you've been preparing for this. "Break!"

We're off to the races now.

CHAPTER 4

Olympic Faith

FAITH FOR THE GOLD

Play #1

"CAN'T STOP, WON'T STOP"

This is it, the moment for which we've been preparing you. It's game time! Your potential faith is no longer in question. Your head is in the game, and you know how to engage your mind over matter to show your opponents the resources you have available. I have no bone in my body that doubts whether your faith will go the distance.

You have manned up and are assured you're not in this game alone. Like those that have played the game before you, even those playing now, you know you are built to last because like them, you've got game.

You are well on your way to championship status! You've learned from Job's saga. The high-level intensity training was no sweat for you because you are confidently ready to play smarter, not harder, becoming a winner with what you have.

***

During the big game you must incorporate all the skills, techniques, and strategies that you've acquired in the conditioning, workout, and training stages. It's time to implement.

Put your faith in action.

This time is where you will see God's will for man.

Yes, even for you, God has a will for your life. All of which can be found in the Word of God.

God's Will for Man Revealed in Scripture

"This is the confidence we have in approaching God: that if we ask anything according to His will, he hears us" (1 John 5:14).

* * *

"He fulfills the desires of those who fear Him; He hears their cry and saves them" (Psalms 145:19).

* * *

"For I know the thoughts that I think toward you, saith the LORD, thoughts of peace, and not of evil, to give you an expected end" (Jeremiah 29:11).

* * *

"Ask and it will be given. Seek and you will find. Knock and the door will be opened" (Matthew 7:7).

* * *

"And receive from Him anything we ask, because we obey His commands and do what pleases Him" (1 John 3:22).

* * *

"Do not be afraid, little flock, for your father has been pleased to give you the kingdom" (Luke 12:32).

* * *

Last year most of the world tuned in to watch the Olympic games. The games were held in Rio de Janeiro. The U.S won one hundred and twenty-one medals overall.

Who really cares about that right? Well, here is something to care about.

We know that the Olympic games occur every four years. This means for four years, athletes of all types, in all regions, are undergoing training even in the off-season. They are constantly training and conditioning themselves to ensure that when the fourth year comes around, they are in winning condition. They're not waiting to get ready. They are getting ready now. Some of the athletes even claim to condition 40 hours a week.

That's an average work week for full-time employees. I find this to be an incredible fact because some non-athletes can barely commit to a 30-minute workout for a day.

It is fascinating that even when they aren't required to train because it's off season, or even when they don't want to practice because they've already played their game, All-Stars come home and work toward the upcoming Olympic year. It's four years out, but they don't stop training, working out, and conditioning.

They do this because their ultimate goal is to win!

Play #2

★ ★ ★

"YOU ARE WHAT YOU EAT"

Even when training in their off season, athletes still ensure to stay healthy by eating right. I find it interesting that all the athletes that competed in the games, no matter what country they were representing or what sport they played, professed that they endured a rigorous and strict diet.

We find that Jairus, in the 5th chapter of Mark reflects this example well. His 12-year-old daughter was sick. He did not falter or fret, he got in the game and ate the Word of God. Just like us Jairus was faced with distractions of many kinds, but he didn't let that stop him. In the thirty sixth verse, he is told, "be not afraid, only believe" (See Mark 5:36; Luke 8:50).

> *You must also know where the promises are.*

Whatever you're standing in faith for, you must believe that it is already created. You must know and believe that! You must also know where the promises are. *"Praise be to the God and Father of our Lord Jesus Christ, who has blessed us in the heavenly realms with every spiritual blessing in Christ"* (Ephesians 1:3). You must also confess what you now know and believe. *"For it is with your heart that you believe and are justified, and it is with your mouth that you confess and are saved"* (Romans 10:10).

If we are to live by faith, we must live by a strict regimen.

God must first confirm His word in your life. You must digest the Word you were given and then put pressure on the Word so that it comes forth in the natural. This causes the situation to change. By doing this, you set the stage for God to be glorified. By doing this, you untie the hands of God and give Him the legal right to get involved in your situation. The doors of possibilities swing open in your life, and you are setup to walk in the blessings of the Lord.

Unlike training day, you are in the game now. There aren't any fictitious scenarios. You are going to face real life challenges. Confessing won't come without opposition.

Circumstances will slowly erode or eat away at your confessions. This is where you will need to stop your natural mental process. Stand still and rehearse the truth. Regurgitate what you have eaten which is God's Word. Speak the truth of God's Word. Through this, you will see the end result of God's power.

"Blessed are those who hunger and thirst after righteousness for they shall be filled" (Matthew 5:6). A strong hunger and deep thirst for your promise will empower you to stay the course. You must be baptized in it. You must be fully convinced and persuaded that this is God's will for your life! Receive the vision for a better life.

Play #3

"KNOWN BY THE COMPANY YOU KEEP"

There are worldly sweets that can interfere with your appetite for the things of God. Synthetic pleasures are drugs, alcohol, food, and the like. You may also face social pleasures, which are desires for educational and community status. Superficial pleasures are the desires for material accumulation. Lastly, there are also soulish pleasures. These are relationships and soul ties you establish during the course of your life.

Some are tempted to give up and throw in the towel because of their social connections. What I want you to keep in mind is that your relationships have a lot to do with your success during the games because they affect your hunger. Relationships come in many different forms. There are parasitic relationships, stigmatic relationships, and democratic relationships.

Parasitic relationships are connections to those people that are bloodsuckers and blackmailers. They rely on others for support and supply. Then there are stigmatic relationships. This connection is with people who see the behaviors of others and label you accordingly. You become known by the company you keep. Democratic relationships are the type of connections where others make the decisions, and you live for the opinions of others.

What you have been created to do won't manifest until you disconnect from the man with your problems and connect with the guy that has your answer. You need to change the crowd you've been following and get with those who are on another level without being intimidated. Stephanie kept confessing it. She wrapped her faith around it and called it in.

Am I stirring you up? I intend to rile you up so much so that your faith takes off and causes you to connect to people who will stretch your mind and give you constructive criticism that causes you to grow. You have expectations, don't you? Have you wrapped your faith around it? Are you flaking out when the going gets rough? I want to remind you to keep believing!

"Hold your head up."

You have successfully come to the end of your faith-building workout. You have what it takes to beat the devil into pieces.

So, hold your tears. Hold your fears. Hold your head up.

Stick your chest out! The time that you've been praying, hoping, and believing for is here. It's time for you to enter the All-Star games and bring home the gold for the Kingdom of God.

The All-Star Prayer

Father God, in the name of Jesus, I thank You. I come before You now desiring that every promise You have placed in my heart comes to pass. Father, I am not satisfied with just blessings when You have already declared Your promises over me. Father, it is my desire that every promise comes to pass in my life, in the name of Jesus. It is my desire that my light will shine so, that even the world will see your good works and glorify You, God.

Father, it is my desire that my needs be met and my dreams be manifested. Father, I thank you now, for manifesting every desire. Father, I thank you now that the blessings of Abraham, the blessings of Isaac, and the blessings of Melchizedeck are upon me in the name of Jesus. Father God, right now, I decree and declare that debt, lack, not enough and insufficiency are cut off from my life in the name of Jesus.

I release the flow, the rivers, prosperity, overflow, riches, fatness, goodness, and thickness, now in the name of Jesus. Let your anointing, let the glory of God, let the wine of God, the wine of prosperity, the wine of goodness, the wine of mercy, and the wine of joy be upon my house and my storehouse now in the name of Jesus.

Father I speak now to the elements. I speak now, to the four winds, and I command them to blow prosperity and favor. I command them to blow promotion and acceleration in the name of Jesus. Blow them in God! I command the four winds to blow; now. I thank you that no hindrance, delay, set back, denial, or cancellation will stand up against your promises manifesting for me. For the race is not given to the swift, nor the battle to the strong, but to he that endures to the end. I am Your All-Star, and because of Your Spirit within me, I will win. It shall be no other way. In Jesus' matchless name, I count it done now. Amen!

ABOUT THE AUTHOR

Dr. Travis Jennings is a necessary leader of our time. He has a dynamic and progressive ministry located in metro Atlanta and has been commissioned to "gather the end-time harvest." For over 16 years, he has faithfully served as the Senior Pastor of The Harvest Tabernacle Church – a ministry that has impacted multiple nations from Canada to South Africa. As an example of a kingdom family, he along with his wife, Executive Pastor Stephanie Jennings and children labor together to lead the growing, thriving, bible-teaching, apostolic, prophetic, multi-racial, mission-driven church.

Dr. Jennings is one of the most prominent leaders today. He is a creative visionary, a passionate kingdom leader, prophetic life coach, prolific orator and a successful author. He is a shrewd entrepreneur, gospel producer and philanthropist who believes the marketplace and ministry have collided and now God's people are set poised to excel and operate in their true authority – in all facets of life.

As a trailblazer, many have experienced total life transformations in their family, personal and professional lives after encountering Dr. Jennings' revolutionary teachings and transparent tutelage. He has successfully cultivated many life-balancing platforms for champions to receive instructions and prophetic navigation for victorious living through multiple community programs and initiatives. Dr. Jennings has authored three books: *The Gathering of Champions*, *Life on Turbo* and *Lifeguard: Help Is on the Way*.

God has called Dr. Jennings to not only serve as Pastor of his local church, but to also assist other Pastors, leaders in government,

81

leaders in education, business leaders as well as those in arts, entertainment and media in order to maximize the call of God upon their lives -- not just in ministry. One tactic he uses to accomplish this is through Harvest Assemblies, a fellowship for pastors who have formally connected with Dr. Travis and Executive Pastor Stephanie Jennings as their spiritual parents. This specific platform serves to cover the pastor and strengthen the local assembly.

His loving relationship with his wife and partner for life, Executive Pastor Stephanie Jennings, serves as a model for marriages around the world. They have five beautiful children – Travis, Briona, Daja, Destiny and David Christopher.